The Japanese

Greg Nickles

CRABTREE
Publishing Company
www.crabtreebooks.com

CRABTREE
Publishing Company

PMB 16A, 350 Fifth Avenue
Suite 3308
New York, NY 10118

612 Welland Avenue
St. Catharines, Ontario
L2M 5V6

Co-ordinating editor: Ellen Rodger
Content editor: Kate Calder
Production co-ordinator: Rosie Gowsell
Assistant editor: Lisa Gurusinghe

Film: Embassy Graphics
Printer: Worzalla Publishing Company

Created by: Brown Partworks Ltd.
Commissioning editor: Anne O'Daly
Project editor: Clare Oliver
Picture researcher: Adrian Bentley
Designer: Dax Fullbrook
Maps: Mark Walker
Consultant: Professor Donald Avery Ph.D, History

CATALOGING-IN-PUBLICATION DATA

Nickles, Greg, 1969-
   The Japanese / Greg Nickles.
   p.cm. – (We Came to North America)
   Includes index.
   ISBN 0-7787-0193-X (RLB) – ISBN 0-7787-0207-3 (pbk.)
   1. Japanese–North America–History–Juvenile literature.
2. Japanese North Americans–History–Juvenile literature.
3. North America–Ethnic relations–Juvenile literature. [1. Japanese North Americans–History. 2. North America–Emigration and immigration.]
I. Title. II. Series.
   E184.J3 N53 2001
   973'.04956–dc21

01-017294
LC

Picture credits

AKG London 22 (top). The Art Archive British Museum 7, back cover; Gunshots 6 (top); Musée des Arts Décoratifs, Paris/Dagli Orti 11. Corbis 10, 25; Bettmann 15, 31 (bottom); Bob Krist 13 (bottom); Joseph Sohm/ChromoSohm Inc. 29 (bottom); Kelly-Mooney Photography 5; Michael S. Yamashita 26 (top), 28 (bottom), 30 (top); Neal Preston 30 (bottom); Nik Wheeler 26 (bottom), 29 (top); Stefano Bianchetti 9; Stephanie Maze 17 (top). Glenbow Archives, Calgary, Canada (NA-1945-1) 4 (top); (NA-3369-1) 16. Hulton Getty 6 (bottom), 12, 17 (bottom), 21 (bottom), 23, 31 (top). Mary Evans Picture Library 19 (bottom). National Archives of Canada (PA-103537) 13 (top); (C 023556) 18; (C-057250) 22 (bottom). North Wind Picture Archives 19 (top). Peter Newark's Pictures 4 (bottom), 20, 21 (top). TRIP C. McCooey title page, 28 (top); M. Jenkin 27.

Cover: Participants in the Japanese American Festival in Japantown, Los Angeles, California, wear Kimonos and traditional Japanese makeup and clothing.

Publishers' credits for eyewitness accounts
page 8: Library of Congress, Manuscript Division, WPA Federal Writers' Project Collection.

page 14: Copyright 1995–2000 Cultural Bridge Productions and Jim Makino.

page 24: Elizabeth Bayley Willis Papers, Acc.2583–6, University of Washington Libraries.

Contents

Introduction

Japanese Americans and Japanese Canadians have lived in North America for over a hundred years. They came to build better lives for themselves and their families. Over the years, they have struggled with **prejudice** and injustice. Japanese Americans and Canadians have built and rebuilt their lives and communities in North America. Today, the Japanese in North America belong to strong, confident, and often very **integrated** communities. Their lifestyle is very different to that of their **ancestors**, most of whom **immigrated** between the 1880s and 1920s.

▲ These immigrants, photographed in 1920, came to Canada from Okinawa in Japan. They settled in Hardieville, Alberta, and found work building the Canadian Pacific Railroad.

The first Japanese immigrants came to Hawaii in 1868 to work on farms before Hawaii was part of the United States. A year later, in 1869, Japanese immigrants came to the United States and set up the Wakamatsu Colony in California. The first Japanese immigrants arrived in Canada and settled in British Columbia in 1877. There are stories of a few Japanese who landed in North America even earlier. They were often sailors who were shipwrecked off the coast of the United States. In fact, the first Japanese to become a U.S. citizen, thirteen-year-old Hikozo Hamada, was rescued from a shipwreck in 1850.

Beginning in the mid-1880s, Japanese came in the tens of thousands, often with the goal of staying for just one year or season to earn extra money. This period of the largest Japanese immigration lasted into the 1920s.

◄ This little girl was put in an internment camp during World War II. Here, she is swearing her allegiance, or loyalty, to the United States.

Japanese Generations

Japanese Americans and Japanese Canadians have a special name for each generation that lives in North America. The first generation, who were born in Japan and later immigrated to North America, are called the *Issei*. Most *Issei* are no longer living. Their children, the second generation, are called the *Nisei*. *Nisei* modified, or changed, the **culture** and traditions of their Japanese ancestors and adopted many North American customs. The *Issei's* grandchildren, the third generation, are called the *Sansei*, the fourth generation is the *Gensei*, and the fifth is the *Yonsei*.

Although many people returned to Japan, many others decided to stay and build a new life in Hawaii or North America.

Japanese immigrants fought against the **racism** of other North Americans during the 1800s and 1900s. At work and in public, they were often poorly treated and not trusted. The worst period was during World War II (1939–1945), when the United States and Canada were at war with Japan. Tens of thousands of Japanese American and Japanese Canadian citizens were put in **internment** camps, not because they had committed crimes, but because they were Japanese. Governments were afraid they would feel more loyalty to their homeland than their new countries. Many Japanese lost the homes and businesses that they had worked so hard to earn. When they were released, they were forced to start their lives all over again.

Despite such hardships, Japanese Americans and Canadians today number about a million strong and are very successful.

▼ **Today, Japanese Americans and Canadians keep their culture alive at celebrations like this Cherry Blossom Parade, held in San Francisco each May.**

A Proud Heritage

Japan is a mountainous island country, in the Pacific Ocean off mainland Asia. It is made up of four main islands and thousands of smaller ones.

Most Japanese trace their roots to peoples from China and Korea who moved to Japan through the Korean Peninsula over 6,000 years ago. They lived in groups called clans that fought constantly over territory. The Yamato clan became dominant around 300 A.D. and encouraged trade with neighboring China. The Japanese borrowed Chinese ideas about religion, art, language, and government. The leader of the Yamato clan became the first **emperor** of Japan.

Over the next thousand years, Japan was controlled by emperors based in the city of Heian, now Kyoto. The empire was split into areas ruled by lords called daimyo, who were served by warrior knights called samurai. Most ordinary people were peasant farmers or tradespeople.

▲ **Samurai fought many wars for their lords, and made decisions that affected all Japanese.**

Family Life

In mid-1800s Japan, most families lived in simple homes, together with children, parents, grandparents, and other relatives. Home life centered around the hearth, which provided heat for cooking and warmth. The family's honor was very important. Everyone obeyed the grandfather, who was head of the family. While men worked outside of the home, women were expected to run the household, caring for children and the elderly.

▶ **A Japanese home, photographed in the 1800s.**

▲ This Japanese illustration shows Commodore Perry's large ship arriving in Japan in 1853.

▼ Japan's four main islands are Honshu, Hokkaido, Shikoku, and Kyushu.

HOKKAIDO

Sea of Japan

HONSHU

Tokyo · Yokohama

Kobe · Kyoto
Hiroshima · · Osaka
SHIKOKU
· Nagasaki
KYUSHU

Pacific Ocean

In the early 1500s, European explorers and traders first reached Japan. At first, Japan's rulers let in foreign goods and Christian **missionaries**, but in 1653, fearing too much foreign influence, they cut off all outside contact. For over 200 years Japanese people were isolated from the world.

Finally, in 1853, U.S. Commodore Matthew C. Perry arrived in Japan leading a fleet of powerful warships and demanded that Japan trade with the United States. The Japanese agreed reluctantly. When Emperor Meiji took over in 1868, Japan quickly opened itself to the outside world. The emperor was determined to make Japan strong by building a modern army and many factories. They were paid for with high taxes placed on farmers and peasants. At the same time, Japan's population boomed. As a result, there were not enough jobs for everyone, and many people did not have enough money to pay their taxes.

Rather than live in poverty, millions of Japanese looked overseas for work and new homes. Many agreed to become contract laborers who travel abroad **temporarily** to earn money. Beginning in the 1880s, thousands of Japanese moved in search of work to mainland Asia, Hawaii, and North and South America.

Eyewitness to History

JOSEPH HECO was born in Komiya, near Osaka, in 1837. At age thirteen, he was shipwrecked in the Pacific Ocean and taken to the United States. Later, he worked as a port official in Japan, because he was able to speak English to traders. Here, he recalls his boyhood in Japan and how his brother's tales gave him an appetite for adventure.

"Komiya was a good-sized village of some four or five hundred houses, with from 2,000 to 2,500 **inhabitants**. The **majority** of its people were farmers; the remainder were fishermen, sailors, and traders.

My brother had always been very fond of **roving**, and at last my stepfather **apprenticed** him at the age of sixteen to his uncle, the captain of a large **junk** trading between Osaka and Yedo. The lad was quick to master his work, and, in a few years' time, had worked himself up to be second officer.

Whenever my brother came home, he used to deliver himself of the story of his travels to the family and to our neighbors. He would tell of his voyages to different places, and of the adventures that had befallen him.

His talk led me to think that if I too could travel, I might be made as much of by the villagers — besides, I thought often and **wistfully** of the different places I could see and the **novel** experiences I could have. Thus, the first thought of rambling crept into my mind, and, from that moment, my desire to leave home never ceased. Yet, I little thought of ever seeing anything beyond my own country; indeed, I don't suppose that, at the time, I even dreamt of the existence of other lands, or if I did, it was to pity the **barbarians** who, I may have heard, came each year or so to Nagasaki to trade with us. "

The Journey

Japanese immigrants left behind family and friends for lands very different from their home. To reach Hawaii and North America, they crossed the Pacific Ocean in crowded ships.

The decision to leave Japan was not an easy one. Japanese immigrants knew they were traveling to a land of strangers with unfamiliar customs and languages. Even the food would be very different from their own. These things made the immigrants feel nervous, so they tried to think instead about the money they would earn for themselves and for their families waiting at home in Japan.

Some Japanese intended to return home as soon as their work contract was finished. Leaving their families was difficult, but they were comforted in knowing they would be reunited in a few months or years. Most immigrants left Japan forever. For them, parting was especially painful.

▲ These immigrants are aboard a ship called the *Shimyo Maru*, which arrived at Angel Island, California, in 1931. The immigration officials are examining the new arrivals before allowing them to come ashore.

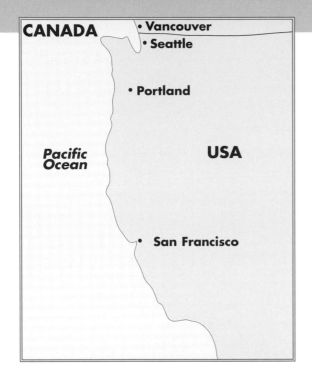

◄ **Japanese immigrants crossed the vast Pacific Ocean to settle in cities on the West Coast.**

From the 1800s to the early 1900s, most Japanese immigrants sailed across the Pacific Ocean aboard large steamships. They crowded into smelly rooms with uncomfortable, dirty bunks. The food served to them on board was bland and in short supply. Illnesses, which could spread quickly onboard ship, were also a problem. People hoped that when they landed, they were healthy enough to find work to earn money.

Most Japanese moved to Hawaii, or to cities along the west coast of North America to work in fishing and farming. Japanese communities grew in ports such as San Francisco, Los Angeles, Portland, and Seattle. Few Japanese traveled far inland, with the exception of the many thousands who went to find work in the huge, thriving city of New York. In Canada, most immigrants landed in British Columbia and settled around the city of Vancouver, along the coast in Tofino, and Prince Rupert, and in the Fraser Valley where they found work in fruit orchards.

◄ **This engraving shows San Francisco in the 1800s, as it was when the first Japanese arrived.**

The Rise and Fall of Immigration

The number of Japanese entering Hawaii and the mainland United States increased from hundreds to more than 400,000 between 1885 and 1924. The number reached 40,000 in Canada. Most of the immigrants were men, but more and more women came starting in the early 1900s. Many migrants left once their work contracts were finished, or because they encountered great prejudice. By the 1920s, about 110,000 had settled on the U.S. mainland and 140,000 in Hawaii, making up a third of Hawaii's population. In the same period, Canada's Japanese population was about 16,000. By 1924, Japanese immigration slowed to a trickle due to racist laws in both countries that restricted and later prevented, immigration from Japan. Even after these laws were lifted in the 1950s and 1960s, the number of Japanese immigrants remained low.

Settling In

Japanese immigrants stayed close together and formed their own communities, mostly because other people were so hostile to them. The thousands of Japanese who decided to settle down rather than return home started their own farms and businesses, and married, and started families.

PERSONS UNDER
20 YRS.
are not allowed
TO ENTER IN THIS PREMISE

READ THIS

▲ This Japanese woman was photographed in Hawaii in 1945. A second-generation settler, she reads an English newspaper.

Life was very hard for the first generation of Japanese who arrived in Hawaii and North America. Many learned that the people who hired them had lied about the working conditions they would find overseas. The Japanese were also frustrated to learn that the basic costs of life were very expensive, so they could not save much of the money they made.

Prejudice was also a problem. People in North America, who were mostly of European ancestry, regarded Asian immigrants as **inferior**. If they hired Japanese, they paid them far less than usual. Outside of work, Japanese were turned away from many stores, churches, and schools.

Despite these hardships, thousands of Japanese decided to remain in Hawaii and North America after completing their first work contracts. People rejected them as neighbors, so they lived side-by-side in their own rural towns, or in the same city neighborhoods. As they slowly saved money, many invested in their own farms and other businesses that supplied their communities with goods and services.

Picture Brides

The thousands of Japanese who immigrated between 1885 and the early 1900s, were mostly young men who came without any family. After the first decade of the 1900s, the U.S. and Canadian governments **restricted** the number of male Japanese immigrants, but allowed more women to come. Many women came to join their husbands or were expected to marry the men already here. About a quarter of those who came were "picture brides." While still in Japan, they exchanged their photographs with Japanese men abroad and arranged a marriage. Their wedding was held in Japan, with another man standing in for the absent groom. The brides then sailed overseas to meet and live with their new husbands.

▲ **These brothers immigrated in 1910. Single men like them often wrote home for a wife.**

By the 1920s, Japanese were well-established in many places throughout Hawaii and the west coast of North America. In the countryside, farmers formed **cooperatives** to help one another ship and market their products. In the cities, they called their neighborhoods *nihonmachi*; in English these were known as "Japantowns" or "Little Tokyos." *Nihonmachi* streets were lined with Japanese businesses, and *Nihonmachi* residents had their own schools. Here, immigrants hardly ever came into contact with non-Japanese people.

▼ **These children in New York gather to watch events at a Japanese Sports Day.**

The Japanese in North America also formed groups to help one another. People from the same region of Japan often formed a *kenjinkai*—a social group where they could meet others and share advice or other support. Temples and churches also brought communities together. They provided important traditional ceremonies for births, marriages, and funerals, in addition to offering classes in English, cooking, and even fashion. Sports leagues for baseball and basketball were also popular among younger people.

Eyewitness to History

JIMMY MAKINO and his wife were *Nisei*, or second-generation Japanese. Jimmy's father and uncle arrived from southern Japan in the early twentieth century. Jimmy describes how his mother was a "picture bride."

" Marriages were **concluded** after letters and photos were typically exchanged between the man in America and his bride-to-be in Japan. My mother, Maketa Toshiye, married my father this way. These marriages, although recognized in Japan, were not recognized in America, so the formal marriage ceremony had to take place immediately after the ship carrying the bride arrived in port.

The lonely Japanese men in America in search of a wife were not always completely honest. It was not uncommon for older men to send photos back to Japan that they had taken years earlier, when they were more attractive. And so, my mother-in-law was shocked when she saw her new husband for the first time because he had aged some eighteen years beyond the likeness of the man she had been expecting to see after her long journey from Japan. Women such as my mother and mother-in-law were known as "picture brides." "

Employment

Japanese immigrants supported themselves in a variety of jobs, such as farming, fishing, and working on the railroads. The immigrants were often offered low-paying, difficult, and sometimes dangerous work that other people did not want.

▲ Japanese farmhands harvest sugar beets in southern Alberta.

The first Japanese contract laborers came to work in the sugarcane **plantations** of Hawaii in 1868, before Hawaii became a state. They worked all day in the hot fields, without breaks, and were whipped by their **overseer** if they slowed down or even talked to one another. At night, groups of workers cooked and slept together in the same room. They were treated little better than criminals.

Many Japanese preferred to do the difficult work on plantations rather than face unemployment and poverty at home. Wages for contract laborers, while low, were still higher than in Japan. Despite the hardships, over the next 50 years, hundreds of thousands of Japanese followed the first plantation laborers to work in Hawaii.

◄ These Japanese American fishermen use traditional bamboo poles to pull fish from the sea.

Many of the Japanese who came to North America found jobs in agriculture. Most had worked on farms in Japan and were experts at **cultivating** rice, fruit, and vegetables. The Wakamatsu Colony, founded in 1869 in California, was the first Japanese farming community on the North American mainland. Instead of tending crops, the Wakamatsu immigrants raised silk worms. Their settlement failed, but the demand for cheap farm labor continued. As immigrants saved money from their jobs, many set up their own farms that produced high **yields**.

Fishing was another industry to which Japanese brought their skills. They bought their own boats and fished off the West Coasts of the United States and Canada. They caught salmon, abalone, and other seafood, which Japanese workers on shore processed.

Some Japanese traveled the continent laying tracks for the railroad companies. Others found work in factories or forestry. In New York, most Japanese worked as sailors, traders, and business people. Many Japanese became doctors, lawyers, dentists, and professors once the racist laws that kept them from holding these professions were removed in the 1950s.

Small Business

Japanese North Americans started many small businesses to serve the needs of their communities. They ran barbershops, boardinghouses, grocery stores, and restaurants that served Japanese foods. For entertainment, they set up pool halls, cafés, and movie houses. People relaxed and chatted with friends at traditional Japanese bathhouses. The owners of these businesses employed many other Japanese to help run them.

▲ Some Japanese served their communities as doctors. This doctor's office was in Hawaii.

Anti-Japanese Feeling

Japanese immigrants suffered terrible discrimination. The cruel insults and injuries they endured were made worse by racist laws passed by the U.S. and Canadian governments.

Japanese immigrants worked tirelessly to become successful and respected members of their communities. They built up their own businesses. With their knowledge of farming and fishing, their work helped their countries' economies grow.

Despite this, many Americans and Canadians refused to accept the Japanese. They distrusted the immigrants and their children simply because they were Asian. Some pressured their politicians to stop all Asians from entering their countries or having rights, such as the right to vote, the right to attend school, or the right to own a fishing license.

In 1882, the U.S. government passed the Chinese Exclusion Act to keep Chinese from entering the country. Employers wanting cheap labor then encouraged the tide of Japanese immigration. The arrival of the Japanese made some people even more angry. Both the United States and Canada allowed few Japanese immigrants in, while at the same time they encouraged millions of European immigrants to settle here.

The Japanese, like many immigrants, lived with abuse and name-calling. While immigrants of European ancestry could blend into a crowd, the physical features of Japanese people made them easy to recognize.

▼ **This Japanese-owned store in Vancouver was damaged during race riots in September 1907.**

18

This photograph shows a court case in San Francisco in 1907. The boy, Keikichi Aoki, is asking to be allowed to attend school, but the principal, Miss Dean, is refusing because he is Japanese.

This racist cartoon from the early-1900s shows President Theodore Roosevelt dreaming about the Japanese, portrayed here as cats, invading the United States.

Just as African Americans were barred from white schools, jobs, neighborhoods, and shops, so too were the Japanese. Many people blamed the Japanese for taking away jobs that would otherwise go to people of European ancestry. They did not take into account that Japanese immigrants created their own jobs, or did work that no one else wanted to do.

In 1906, the U.S. government passed a law that kept people born in Japan from becoming U.S. citizens. The U.S. and Canadian governments strictly controlled the numbers of Japanese immigrants. In 1924, the U.S. Immigration Act stopped Japanese immigration nearly altogether. Canada followed suit in 1928 by limiting Japanese immigration to 150 people per year.

Even with such strict controls, hatred of the Japanese continued. During World War II (1939-1945), Japanese immigration was stopped entirely. It was years before Japanese Americans and Canadians received recognition for their achievements. Prejudice against them increased until the 1950s and 1960s, when most of the racist laws and immigration quotas were finally **reversed**.

The Bombing of Pearl Harbor

On December 7, 1941, Japan's military made a surprise attack on the U.S. naval base at Pearl Harbor, Hawaii. During the war with Japan that followed, the U.S. and Canadian governments forced thousands of North American Japanese into prison camps.

▲ **This propaganda magazine cover from 1938, depicts a Japanese man as an enemy spy taking pictures.**

Several years before the attack on Pearl Harbor, Japan's powerful army battled throughout eastern Asia. The Japanese army brutally attacked and took over large parts of the mainland and many Pacific islands. Anti-Japanese feeling in North America grew. It increased again when World War II broke out in Europe in 1939, and Japan made a **pact** with Germany to conquer large parts of the world.

Canada, a member of the British Commonwealth, immediately joined the war, but the United States did not. Japanese leaders thought that U.S. military bases on nearby Pacific islands posed a threat to Japan. As a result, Japan bombed Pearl Harbor in December 1941. The next day, the United States declared war on Japan.

The attack on Pearl Harbor was a shock to Americans and terrible news for the thousands of first, second, and third-generation Japanese living in Hawaii and North America. They worried about friends and relatives in their homeland, but they were also loyal to the United States and Canada, where they had built new lives.

In the Armed Forces

▲ These Japanese American soldiers who served in Italy during World War II received awards for bravery.

Many Japanese Americans and Canadians had fought bravely for their countries in World War I (1914–1918). In 1941, after the attack at Pearl Harbor, the military rejected Japanese as soldiers. In 1943, the U.S. government changed its **policy** and formed a special Japanese American battalion called the 442nd Infantry Regimental Combat Team. Many men joined to prove that Japanese Americans were loyal to the United States. They earned a record number of medals for their bravery in battle. Despite their heroism, 442nd veterans still suffered prejudice after the war.

Once the war broke out, people questioned the loyalty of Japanese Americans and Canadians, even though most children of the immigrants had never been to Japan.

Many people saw all Japanese as enemies, and were convinced they would become spies or **saboteurs** for the Japanese Empire. They unfairly blamed people of Japanese ancestry for **atrocities** committed by the Japanese military. In 1942, many North Americans demanded the Japanese in North America be arrested.

▼ Japan's surprise attack on the Pearl Harbor naval base left U.S. warships ablaze.

Although there was no evidence that people of Japanese ancestry would commit any crimes, North American leaders listened to accusations instead of facts. They ordered that Japanese American and Canadian men, women, and children be **relocated** to bleak internment camps, far from their coastal homes. Most were forced to remain there until the war ended in 1945. Japanese Americans in Hawaii were not forced to move to camps because they made up almost half the population of the state.

The Wartime Internment Camps

Thousands of Japanese Americans and Canadians were humiliated by their imprisonment during World War II. Once released, many discovered that they had lost the savings, property, and businesses they had worked so hard to earn.

▲ Japanese Americans line up at an internment camp in California.

▼ Japanese families board a train for a camp in British Columbia.

Japan's attack on Pearl Harbor marked a terrible turning point for Japanese in North America. The years of growing prejudice from other North Americans suddenly erupted into mass arrests of Japanese Americans and Canadians. Even though they were loyal to the United States and Canada, Japanese families were rounded up by police and sent to internment camps. People tried to make these actions sound less extreme by calling the camps "relocation" or "isolation" centers. The camps were no better than prisons surrounded by barbed wire fences and watched by armed guards with orders to shoot **escapees**.

Most internment camps were stationed away from the West Coast where the Japanese lived, because of fears that the prisoners might help the Japanese military invade the coast. Families were divided between different camps, and it was years before some prisoners saw their friends and loved ones again.

Many U.S. camps were old army barracks. In Canada, camps were set up in abandoned towns and on vast prairie farms. People were given only basic provisions including a few clothes, plain food, and poorly built quarters.

▲ The Japanese American owner of this store put up this sign on the day after the attack on Pearl Harbor.

Many interned Japanese were crowded into small, dirty rooms that were freezing cold in the winter and hot and dusty in the summer. During the day, many were forced to work on farms, while others were left to boredom.

The internment devastated Japanese communities on the West Coast. When they were released, many detainees returned to their homes and businesses to find them taken over by other people. In British Columbia, the government had sold their property for a fraction of its value. The Japanese had to begin rebuilding their lives from scratch.

In the years after the war, Japanese people in North America have won millions of dollars in compensation from their governments for their suffering in the war. During the 1980s, both the U.S. and Canadian governments issued formal apologies to their citizens of Japanese ancestry.

Starting Over

Rather than rebuild the communities and businesses they had on the West Coast before World War II, many Japanese Americans and Canadians chose to resettle across the continent to the east. Scarred by their time in internment camps, they often distanced themselves from traditional Japanese culture, and tried to fit in with the white, English-speaking majority. Thousands of others could not put aside their pain and anger at being imprisoned. They left North America forever to live in Japan.

Eyewitness to History

This is part of a letter from a Japanese boy staying at a camp during World War II. It was written to ELIZABETH BAYLIS WILLIS, his English teacher back home in Seattle.

" The barracks with their rooms were not what I expected them to be, but they are comfortable enough. It is a framework of wood with **shiplap** over it. The walls between the rooms don't quite reach the ceiling, and if one talks loudly he can be heard at the other end of the barrack. In each room, there is a woodstove, which takes care of the heating problem, for, in the morning and night, it gets quite cold.

We've hung curtains and drapes, made our own furniture, and have tried to make our room as much as possible like home. Everything is a little crude, but it's all right, for a little crudeness fits into the picture. It's a place for old clothes and boots, because, when it rains, the streets get muddy, and, when it becomes hot, you eat a lot of dust, so the boys say.

There are six **mess halls,** and, when it's time to eat, we line up outside. By the time the doors open, there is a very long line, so the early birds eat first. The food is all right but I think I could stand a little more, and, as always, it could be better.

The place is entirely surrounded by a barbed wire fence, and soldiers watch on towers and march back and forth along the fence. Sometimes we talk to them and they are friendly. I don't mind them watching me, and I believe that the others don't mind either. Everyone seems to be contented and have adapted themselves to the change, even though many things are lacking. "

Japanese Culture

Today, many Japanese Americans and Canadians no longer speak the language or follow and customs of their ancestors. They remain proud of their **heritage** and Japanese communities across North America promote many of their traditions to keep them alive.

▼ The presentation of food is an important part of Japanese cuisine.

Most Japanese Americans and Canadians speak English. They dress, behave, and live like other North Americans, but their traditional culture is not lost. Parents and grandparents remember their Japanese traditions and continue to celebrate them. Community centers organize classes, concerts, and gatherings.

Some parts of Japanese culture have been adopted throughout North America. Japanese food, for example, is very popular. Sushi is served at Japanese restaurants in many cities. Sushi are small rolls of rice and seaweed paper topped with seafood and vegetables. Sake, which is a rice wine, is a popular traditional drink.

▲ At this school in Hawaii, children learn to play traditional Japanese instruments.

The Japanese have also contributed to the art of gardening. Immigrants tended the first successful flower farms on the West Coast, and also introduced Japanese varieties of trees, such as gingko, persimmon, and wisteria. The famous cherry trees in Potomac Park in Washington, D.C., were a gift from the Japanese city of Tokyo. **Bonsai** trees are also highly prized. These special plants must be carefully pruned, to shape them into perfectly formed, miniature trees.

► The tea garden in San Francisco, California, is one of the most beautiful examples of a Japanese garden in the world.

Japanese martial arts are very popular. Many people study karate, an ancient form of self-defense that uses swift kicks and punches. Jujitsu is a form of hand-to-hand combat, once used by Japan's samurai warriors. In the 1800s, Dr. Jigoro Kano adapted this art into the sport called judo. Both jujitsu and judo are forms of unarmed combat, but students of judo try to defeat an opponent without doing harm.

Shiatsu is a traditional Japanese method of healing that is widely practiced in North America. A therapist pushes pressure points on the body, in order to stimulate the flow of energy and improve **circulation**.

At cultural centers across North America, people work to keep other Japanese traditions alive. Students learn origami, the art of folding colored paper to form shapes and animals. Japanese calligraphy is also practiced. It is a type of elegant writing done with a paintbrush. People also read and write short **haiku** poems.

Religions

Some people of Japanese ancestry in North America still follow Japan's ancient, traditional religions, called Shinto and Buddhism. Shinto, which means "way of the gods," originated in Japan long ago. In return for simple favors and blessings, worshippers leave offerings of food and prayers to the many Shinto gods, called *kami*, that live throughout nature. Buddhism is based on the teachings of the Buddha, a **philosopher** who encouraged people to use **meditation** and wisdom to find peace and happiness. Many Japanese Americans and Canadians embrace Christian customs and beliefs. Christianity is the religion based on the teachings of Jesus Christ, who Christians believe is the son of God. The teachings are written in the holy book called the Bible. Christianity was first introduced to the Japanese by Western missionaries who visited Japan almost 500 years ago.

Japanese Festivals

Throughout the year, members of the Japanese community celebrate traditional festivals with colorful costumes, music, and dance. They have also adopted many festivals of European origin.

Many North Americans of Japanese heritage are of mixed race, because their parents married non-Japanese. Over the years, they have adopted festivals and other celebrations of North America. Japanese communities are very proud of their traditional festivals known as *matsuri*.

Many Japanese festivals are local events that celebrate special occasions within the community. Japanese temples and churches set up festive bazaars with rows of vendors. Towns or neighborhoods hold fairs with rides and games.

The biggest occasion on the Japanese calendar is New Year's Day, which the Japanese call *Oshogatsu*. Families and friends gather to throw a huge party and eat traditional food and drink. The menu for Japanese New Year is very specific. Each item of food has symbolic importance, and missing even one food is said to bring bad luck.

▲ **Carp-shaped kites mark Children's Day. The carp's struggle upriver symbolizes the struggle through life.**

◄ **A little girl pours tea over a statue of the Buddha. This is one of the rituals performed to celebrate *Hana Matsuri*, Buddha's birthday.**

A proper *Oshogatsu* meal must include sushi, boiled vegetables, teriyaki, and tempura. Teriyaki is a type of marinated meat and tempura is a dish of deep-fried vegetables and shrimp. Many other foods are served, including long soba noodles that **symbolize** long life.

The Doll Festival, called *Hina Matsuri*, is held on March 3. On this day, little girls display fifteen traditional dolls on a set of platforms, called a *hina-dan*. The dolls represent the Japanese emperor, empress, and the royal court. The girls wear their best clothes or a **kimono** and serve the dolls food and drink.

On Children's Day in May, parents traditionally prayed for their sons to have successful lives. Today, all children eat special sweet bean and rice cakes and fly kites shaped like carp fish. These are symbols designed to bring the children bravery, strength, and determination.

In July, *Tanabata* honors the legend of two stars that fell in love, but only saw each other twice a year because they sat on opposite sides of the sky. People go to poetry readings and hang strips of paper from tree branches as symbols of poetry.

In July and August, *Bon Odori* honors the spirits of ancestors with parades, music, and dancing at Buddhist temples. After three days of celebrating, people float small paper lanterns on rivers which are said to guide the spirits back to heaven.

▲ **Girls wear their best kimonos for the Cherry Blossom Festival.**

◄ **The *Nisei* Week parade takes place each August in Little Tokyo, Los Angeles.**

29

Here to Stay

Many American and Canadian politicians, actors, scientists, artists, and businesspeople share Japanese ancestry. They have made their mark at home and internationally.

Since World War II, many people of Japanese ancestry have risen to public attention for their great achievements. Some of the most influential have been state and national politicians. They have helped win important rights for the Japanese community, in addition to providing good government to non-Japanese people. George Ryochi Ariyoshi is one of the best known. Elected governor of Hawaii for three **consecutive** terms beginning in 1974, he became the first Japanese American state governor. Dan Ken Inouye of Hawaii, a former soldier in the 442nd Regimental Combat Team, became the first Japanese American elected to Congress in 1959. He lost an arm defending his country as a soldier in World War II.

Activists such as Tsuyako "Sox" Kitashima, Mike Masaoka, and Edison Uno also helped win recognition and fairer treatment for Japanese Americans.

Politicians and activists have probably made the biggest impact on people's lives, but it is actors and athletes who are often more recognizable. Pat Morita, whose real first name is Noriyuki, is famous for his roles in the *Happy Days* television show from the 1970s and the *Karate Kid* films of the 1980s. Kristi Yamaguchi, a figure skater, became famous on the ice rinks of World Championships and at the 1992 Winter Olympics, where she won the gold medal. Born and raised in California, Yamaguchi overcame club feet, a condition that deforms the feet, as a young child before she learned to skate. She won her Olympic gold medal when she was just twenty years old and now skates in professional shows and competitions.

North Americans of Japanese heritage have become famous artists and writers. Architect Minoru Yamasaki (1912-1986) and sculptor Isamu Noguchi (1904-1988) are just two of the many Japanese who have worked in the visual arts.

▲ **This giant, stunning sculpture stands in New York. It is the work of the American artist, Isamu Noguchi, whose father was Japanese.**

▼ **Figure skater Kristi Yamaguchi at the 1992 Winter Olympics.**

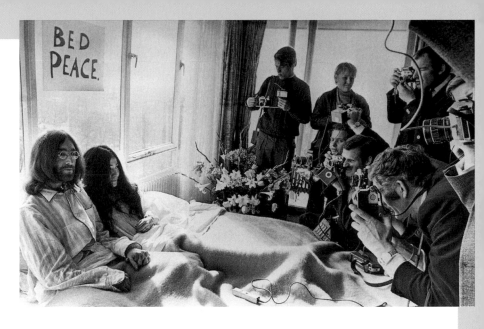

Yamasaki and Noguchi designed stark, modern structures in New York and other cities.

Joy Kogowa is a celebrated author, poet, and activist who has often written of her personal experiences in a World War II internment camp in Canada. She became involved in the movement to get the Canadian government to make amends for its shameful treatment of Japanese Canadians during World War II. Kogowa's book *Obason* tells of a family's life in an internment camp and the lasting pain of that experience, from a young girl's point of view.

Other people of Japanese heritage have risen to fame for different reasons. Manzo Nagano was the first Japanese to settle in Canada, in 1877. In his honor, the Canadian government named a peak in British Columbia "Mount Nagano," in 1977. Lieutenant Colonel Ellison S. Onizuka realized his lifelong dream and became the first Japanese American astronaut, flying into space aboard the shuttle *Discovery*, in 1985. Sadly, Onizuka died the next year aboard the shuttle *Challenger*, when it exploded in flight.

▲ **Japanese American Yoko Ono found fame as an experimental artist, but her name became known around the world after her marriage to Beatles star John Lennon, in 1969.**

World-class Scientist

Dr. David Suzuki is an expert **geneticist**, a world-leading environmental activist, and one of the most famous people in Canada. He was born in 1936 to Japanese parents in British Columbia. As a child, he was interned with his parents during World War II. After graduating from school, Suzuki pursued work in science as well as radio and television broadcasting in which he hosted several educational programs. He has also brought many environmental causes to the attention of people around the world. For his tireless work, he has received awards from UNESCO and the United Nations, as well as many other honors.

▲ **David Suzuki brought science to a wider audience.**

Glossary

ancestor Family member from the past, such as a great grandparent.

apprentice To learn a trade.

atrocities Terrible actions.

barbarians Uncivilized people.

bonsai The art of growing tiny trees to look like full-size ones.

circulation The flow of blood around the body.

concluded Completed.

consecutive Following each other.

cooperative An organization that shares labor and profits.

culture A group of people's way of life, including their language, beliefs, and art.

cultivating Growing crops.

discrimination Unfair treatment, on the grounds of race, sex, or religion.

emperor The ruler of a very large territory.

escapee A person trying to escape.

geneticist Someone who studies human genes.

haiku A three-line Japanese poem that does not rhyme.

heritage The language, beliefs, lifestyles, and art that people receive from previous generations.

immigrate Come to settle in one country from another country.

inferior Lower; not so important.

inhabitant Someone who lives in a place permanently.

integrate When people of all races or ethnic groups come together without restriction.

internment Confinement or imprisonment.

junk A flat-bottomed East Asian ship with large, square sails.

kimono A loose, Japanese robe, tied with a sash called an obi.

majority Largest part or group.

meditation Quiet, deep thought.

mess hall The place where a large group of people eat together.

missionaries Religious people who work to change other people's religious beliefs to their own.

novel New and unusual.

overseer Supervisor or boss.

pact An agreement.

philosopher Someone who studies the reasons for human existence and ways of thinking and behaving.

plantation Estate on which a crop, such as sugarcane, is grown and which requires cheap labor.

policy A course of action.

prejudice An unfair opinion.

racism Belief that some races are better or worse than others.

relocate To move from one place to another.

restrict To limit.

reversed To revoke or change to an opposite direction.

roving Traveling around.

saboteur Someone who works within a nation on behalf of its enemy by destroying equipment.

shiplap Overlapping boards.

symbolize Something that represents something else. A flag symbolizes a country.

temporarily For a short time.

wistfully With longing.

yield The amount of produce that a farm makes.

Index

1 2 3 4 5 6 7 8 9 0 Printed in the USA 5 4 3 2 1